Original title:
Echoes in the Living Room

Copyright © 2025 Creative Arts Management OÜ
All rights reserved.

Author: Dean Whitmore
ISBN HARDBACK: 978-1-80587-200-9
ISBN PAPERBACK: 978-1-80587-670-0

The Last Sip of Tea

The kettle sings its final tune,
As I sip the remnants of the afternoon.
The biscuit crumbles, oh what a scene,
A mouthful of crumbs, and I feel quite keen.

Laughter drips like honey, sweet,
With my cat plotting a daring repeat.
A leap and a bound, paws on the chair,
These moments of joy are beyond compare.

Cracks in the Walls of Time

Pictures hang wonky, crooked and free,
Those eyes once darting, now stare at me.
A clock ticks loudly, mocking my plight,
Is it morning or evening? What's wrong, daylight?

Dust bunnies gather, they form a great troop,
In their secret conference, they plan a grand scoop.
"Let's surprise the humans with a sudden chase!"
And as they glide by, I laugh in this space.

Glistening Dust Motions

Sunlight bursts forth, a spotlight for dust,
They dance in the air, their moves are a must.
Like tiny performers, they twist and sway,
Waltzing through sunbeams, come what may.

I grab for a napkin, ready to fight,
But they swirl away, full of sheer delight.
Who knew a speck could take me for five?
My living room circus thrives to survive.

The Taste of Remembrance

A half-finished puzzle lies on the floor,
Grandma's old stories sneak in through the door.
With each missing piece, I burst into glee,
Her laughter echoes, inviting me to tea.

A snack from the past, a cookie so bright,
It crumbles like memories shared in the night.
The sweet and the savory blend in my mind,
Each taste a reminder, of love intertwined.

Frame by Frame

In the corner, a picture speaks,
Whispering tales of silly weeks.
A cat in a hat, oh what a sight,
Dancing around in pure delight.

Grandma's glasses sit on the floor,
Laughing at life, wanting more.
The frames wiggle with each funny quirk,
A silent show, a joyful work.

Conversations with the Past

The old chair creaks, it joins the chat,
Telling stories of this and that.
A sock puppet appears on cue,
Quipping a tale, quite absurd too.

Know the lamp with its wobbly base?
Stealing the light, it joins the race.
"Who needs a candle?" it winks and laughs,
Transforming the room with glowing gaffs.

The Unseen Presence

The dust bunnies play hide and seek,
Tickling toes as I start to peek.
They giggle softly, it seems to me,
In this soft glow, they dance with glee.

A ghost of laughter, floating by,
Mimicking whispers, oh me, oh my!
With every creak, the fun resumes,
A party of poltergeists in vacuums.

Windowsill Chronicles

On the windowsill, a mug sits proud,
Holding the secrets of speeches loud.
Bad jokes and riddles, steaming with glee,
Spilling the beans between you and me.

A cactus nods with its prickly grin,
Joining the banter as we break in.
Sunbeams sprinkle; the curtains sway,
While laughter echoes the joy of the day.

Unraveled Threads of Laughter

In a chair that squeaks and groans,
A tale unfolds of socks and phones.
Whispers of mishaps fill the air,
As I search for a snack with only despair.

Cats on the couch, plotting their schemes,
While I trip on toys, chasing my dreams.
The dog steals the show, with a goofy face,
As I stumble through this comical space.

Time Travel Through Coffee Cups

With each sip, I'm back in time,
To when I rhymed my life in mime.
A mug in hand, adventures spring,
Coffee wizardry, I can't help but sing.

Tea stains tell tales of laughter and woes,
Each mug reveals what nobody knows.
I raise a toast to yesterday's brew,
If only this cup could hold the true view.

The Sound of Forgotten Days

Old records spin with a playful creak,
Memories dance, and giggles peak.
Dust bunnies waltz on the wooden floor,
Inviting me back to the comedy store.

Laughter lingers like a warm embrace,
Floating through corners, a vibrant trace.
In these walls, stories gently sway,
Reminding me of the whimsy of play.

Murmurs in the Air

Chairs whisper secrets of yesterday's fun,
When I mistakenly called my dog "Son."
Walls chuckle softly, sharing the glee,
Of my antics with laundry and spilled iced tea.

The sunbeam's a spotlight on feeble jokes,
As playful spirits tease like friendly folks.
With laughter woven in the fabric of space,
This room's a circus, a joyful place!

Conversations with Ghosts

In the corner, chairs do sway,
As laughter dips, then skips away.
Phantoms argue, toss their shades,
Jokes are lost in spectral parades.

Muffled whispers fill the air,
Telling tales of worn-out chairs.
"Is that your sock?" one ghost will tease,
"Only if you'll share my cheese!"

Moments freeze, then come alive,
A ghostly drink, they will contrive.
"Did you hear that? Or was it me?"
"Just the cat, or so I see."

As old jokes tumble, take a spin,
With playful spirits, let's begin.
In this room where none can stay,
We all join in the ghostly play.

Memory's Silent Symphony

Upon the wall, an old clock ticks,
Grinding time with funny tricks.
It strikes a pose, like it's not aware,
Of all the laughter floating there.

With memories like flickering lights,
Dancing shadows on the nights.
Each giggle soft, but sharp enough,
To tease the heart, it's just good stuff.

Socks and slippers in a race,
One ghost trips, then steals a space.
"Keep it down! The neighbors scream!"
"Just a joke—don't break the dream!"

Yet in the chaos, songs arise,
With laughter flashing in our eyes.
This room plays tunes, a silent show,
Where every memory learns to glow.

The Faintest Reverb

In the space where laughter lingers,
A clumsy ghost shakes all the fingers.
"Oops, not me!" it shrieks then winks,
As I pour tea, it smiles and blinks.

Chairs creak softly with delight,
In this hush where jokes take flight.
A whistle here, a pop there too,
"Did you just hear a ghostly 'boo'?"

Toast flies high, and so does jam,
An errant spirit? Yes, I am!
They steal a bite, I roll my eyes,
In this charade, they win the prize.

Yet in the warmth of shared surprise,
We gather 'round with no goodbyes.
With every jest, the spirits play,
And leave me chuckling through the day.

Voices Beneath the Surface

Underneath the table, lost socks hide,
While friendly ghosts take joy in pride.
"Is that where you keep your snacks?"
"Of course not! It's for the facts!"

Chortling echoes, gentle yet clear,
Each story brings another cheer.
With rolling eyes and playful jibes,
We bowl over tales, where fun imbibes.

In the kitchen, pots do rattle,
While spirits dance with merry prattle.
"Who's making that mess?" a voice protests,
"It wasn't me; I'm just a guest!"

Thus, the night rolls on so bright,
In this symphony of pure delight.
With laughter bounding, ghosts take wing,
The living room turns to a fun-filled spring.

Remnants of Laughter's Glow

In the corner sits a chair,
Worn down by tales we would share.
A cat's meow interrupts the flight,
Of stories spun late into the night.

The coffee spills, a mark on the rug,
A dance complete with a silly shrug.
Memory borders on ridiculous threads,
As we argue who's turning more reds.

Candles flicker, shadows dance,
Through the clutter, we find our chance.
With every chuckle that fills the air,
The laughter finds places to declare.

Worn shoes kicking dust on the floor,
We leap over each memory's door.
Oh, laughter lingers like a sweet tune,
Lighting the room like a jester's balloon.

Reverberations of Time Passed

Polaroids cling to the fridge door,
Prompting a giggle from days of yore.
Frosted cakes and messy pies,
The kitchen still hums with our wild cries.

We'd shout and burp till the sun set,
Making promises we would never regret.
A misplaced sock in the laundry's heart,
Each woven memory a quirky art.

The old clock chimes with a silly sound,
Time flips like a burger turned around.
In an orchestra of clatter and lace,
We find our rhythm, our own embrace.

Old chairs squeak at the improper jokes,
As laughter tumbles like playful folks.
Time lost here is a jest that's free,
Wrapped in the moments, just you and me.

Ghosts of Conversations Past

Chairs gossip with quiet squeaks,
Where friendship blossoms and laughter tweaks.
Old mugs whisper of secrets spilled,\nTheir humor sweet and warmly filled.

The ceiling fan nods as tales unfold,
While dust motes dance, their stories bold.
Each word lingers, fluttering away,
Like tossing a coin to the whims of the day.

We recall the days of feigned grumps,
And how chairs were chosen for the bumps.
Two friends in battle with popcorn fights,
Much laughter escapes into the nights.

Even shadows break into a cheer,
Every murmur engraved, crystal clear.
Moments twirl in a playful swirl,
Ghosts of the past in memories unfurl.

The Silent Hum of Nostalgia

A remote control takes a lazy glance,
Not ready to change from our goofy dance.
When TV shows played in sitcom glee,
We'd laugh so loud, just you and me.

The couch grooves where our bodies lay,
Not stitched, but sewn with words we say.
A blanket fort of inside jokes,
Holding treasure from all the pokes.

Invisible strings tug at the seams,
Of bygone days stitched into dreams.
Whiskered moments hide in the seams,
Of laughter's echoes and playful themes.

Oh, how the past gives a wink and a nod,
In each chuckle, a sparkle of odd.
With every convulsion of joy we find,
Living rooms pulse with memories intertwined.

Flickering Memories

In the corner, a shadow bounces,
The cat is now posing, king of the couches.
Grandpa's jokes bounce off the walls,
As laughter erupts and the dust lightly calls.

The plant on the ledge seems to listen,
While crumbs from the snack make the floor glisten.
A dance-off erupts by the coffee table,
Pretzel-stretching champs, oh so unstable.

A game of charades turns into a mime,
We trip over rug just to make it sublime.
Each giggle a tick, each snort a delight,
Perfectly silly, our joy takes flight.

Once just a room, now a time machine,
Where goofy moments are forever seen.
Memories flicker, laugh lines grow wide,
In this cozy nook, our hearts abide.

Moments Stilled in Grace

The clock ticks slow, though we are in haste,
Each second a snapshot, none going to waste.
The sofa, our stage, for games that we play,
Improv and giggles light up the day.

A spilled drink becomes a memory grand,
We laugh, we clap, just a little unplanned.
The popcorn fights flying high through the air,
A toast to the fun — no moment gets spare.

Like a photo freeze, all silly and bright,
Moments of chaos glow softly in light.
The couch becomes magic, transforming our fate,
As laughter rolls in, we just can't be late.

Grace in the madness, joy in the mess,
In every misstep, there's laughter to bless.
Time stands still as we stretch and we grin,
Moments of grace, fun memories begin.

Remnants of Warmth

In this place, once a riot, a skirmish for snacks,
With crumbs of our laughter strewn over the tracks.
Blankets lie tangled, a fort made of cheer,
As siblings recount every sneeze and each tear.

The coffee mug smiles, worn from the dent,
Holding tales of the nights when we all just went bent.
A whisper of spice from the old dinner night,
Spaghetti as weapons, oh, what a sight!

Sticky hands gather to find hidden treats,
The chase for the dessert, a dance with quick feats.
The couch an old friend, a corner of bliss,
Where each laugh and quirk becomes hard to miss.

In this room of our hearts, warmth carries the glow,
Remnants of joy linger sweet and aglow.
No artifact here is just out of place,
Each silly refrain marks a memory's trace.

The Soul of a Space

This room spins stories, treasure-filled tracks,
Where laughter and chaos conspire in packs.
A puzzle of pictures hangs over the chair,
Each face and each smile tells of our care.

Underneath cushions, old treasures abound,
A stray sock, a toy, the world's funniest sound.
The DOG - oh wait, it's just Uncle Bob's snore,
What's adventure without just a little bit more?

With feet on the table, we lounge in delight,
The popcorn bowl's empty, we snuggle up tight.
The couch groans in comfort, its back with a sigh,
As stories unfold, the hours just fly by.

In this crazy realm where time does defy,
Bubbles of joy float and twinkle with pride.
The soul of this space, a love song we weave,
With silly old moments, we never want to leave.

Tables Set for Time Travelers

In a chair from a century past,
I sip tea that's oddly vast.
The biscuit crumbles, oh what a scene,
I wonder if this was vintage cuisine.

A fork made of silver, a knife of gold,
I think they must've been very bold.
Each nibble's a journey, a laugh to unfold,
Time bends around as stories are told.

The clock ticks backward, time feels odd,
Each tick makes my head give a nod.
A voice from the future hollers, "Stay still!"
Yet I can't resist the thrill of the spill!

So here we gather, the lost and the found,
Dancing on beams without making a sound.
Future and past, we're losing the grind,
Who knew that time travelers could be so unrefined?

The Breath of Familiarity

The couch creaks under the weight of the years,
It whispers stories and shares all our fears.
With popcorn scattered like confetti in spring,
A laugh erupts when the antics take wing.

The cat jumps up as if on cue,
Decides it's time to steal the view.
While the TV blares a nostalgic tune,
We're lost in our thoughts, high as a balloon.

Old magazines piled, a fortress of dreams,
Each page turns softly, or so it seems.
We chuckle at styles that never should've returned,
And battle over whose toast got burned.

With a wink and a nod, we all raise a glass,
To the moments that linger and those that pass.
In the air thick with smiles, we seize the day,
Familiarity's breath is our grand ballet.

Nightfall Whisperings

As night creeps in, the shadows play,
A game of charades with the light on display.
Candles flicker like lost fireflies,
Illuminating giggles, oh my, how time flies!

In the corner, a stack of board games awaits,
The dice spin wildly, rewriting our fates.
Laughter erupts over misplayed moves,
As victory dances and mischief grooves.

The fridge hums a tune, a melody rare,
With leftovers reminiscing of culinary flair.
We toast to the night with cups piled high,
And recount old tales that make us sigh.

As the clock ticks on, and eyelids droop,
We gather our dreams in a cozy troop.
With one last chuckle, we drift into sleep,
Nightfall whispers secrets, our hearts to keep.

A Room Where Time Stands Still

In a chair where laughter's caught,
Socks and sandals, oh, what a lot!
Cookies on the ceiling fan,
Wonder how that even ran.

With a cat that thinks he's king,
Swatting shadows, what a fling!
Cushions bounce like they have wings,
Oh, the joy this chaos brings!

Dust bunnies dance in silly glee,
Chasing dreams of grand confetti.
Look, a spill of soda flies,
While sprightly birds just laugh and sigh.

In this room, the clock's a joke,
Ticking slow and feeling broke.
Laughter wraps the air so tight,
In this timeless, funny flight.

Traces of Yesterday's Joy

Crumbs from snacks hide in the seams,
Whispers of our wildest dreams.
Pillows hold our secrets tight,
As the sun dips, oh what a sight!

Marshmallow fights and popcorn rain,
Remnants of our silly pain.
Footprints stain the carpet bright,
Echoing our playful plight.

Jars of giggles, piles of fun,
Who knew chaos could be run?
A dance-off with the vacuum loud,
All in all, we feel so proud.

As night falls, the laughter swells,
Stories tangled, like old spells.
In the glow of fading light,
We count our joys, our hearts take flight.

Conversations with the Walls

Oh, the walls have tales to tell,
Of midnight snacks and silly spells.
They've heard our secrets, loud and clear,
And chuckled softly through each cheer.

The paint peels like an old friend's grin,
While chairs get ready for the din.
Curtains sway like gossip queens,
Enthralled by our crazy routines.

Lamps wink like they know the score,
As we debate who dropped the ore.
The radio hums a silly tune,
While we dance under the lazy moon.

Oh, the memories soaked in cheer,
Speculation fills each ear.
In this quirky, comfy pace,
Even the walls join in the race.

The Stillness Between Heartbeats

In the quiet gaps we find,
A giggle hides, a word unkind.
Moments pause like breathless sighs,
Time tickles us, and laughter flies.

The clock stands still, a playful tease,
As we dance with the cheeky breeze.
Game nights turn to chaos bold,
Tales of glory, brave and old.

In this calm, the jokes ignite,
Tickling bones with sheer delight.
Stories swirl like fluffy clouds,
Muffled giggles in small crowds.

As we sit, the world spins slow,
Comfort found in jest and flow.
In heartbeats shared and joyful sound,
These fleeting bits of life abound.

Reminiscence of a Single Portrait

A painting hangs, a smirk so sly,
It seems to wink as I pass by.
With every glance, it whispers tales,
Of family feuds and doggy trails.

That face from years, so stiff and grand,
A pose that surely wasn't planned.
I swear it moved, just last week,
Or was that my wine? Perhaps I'm weak.

The dog stole socks, the cat kept watch,
While grandpa dreamed of being a botch.
It's funny how the past can play,
In this little room, night turns to day.

So here I sit, my heart so light,
With painted smiles to share the night.
Each glance recalls a silly spree,
In the living room of memory.

Footsteps on the Wooden Floor

The floorboards creak, a rhythmic song,
I tiptoe quiet, but it feels so wrong.
A sneaky snack, just a crumb or two,
Yet the squeaks betray me, a noisy zoo.

Each step I take is a whisper bold,
Like marching bands with secrets told.
I leap and dance, afraid to trip,
While shadows watch my sneaky slip.

The cat rolls by, with eyes so sly,
Chasing after ghosts that flutter by.
We tip-tap laugh, what a silly sight,
As the living room unveils the night.

So I'll laugh loud, let my heart soar,
For every creak there's a tale galore.
In footsteps bright, we find our cheer,
As whispers and giggles fill the sphere.

The Weight of Unsaid Goodbyes

The clock ticks loud, a sly little tease,
As I delay my leaving with a breeze.
Goodbye looms large like an awkward dance,
And here comes fate, not leaving to chance.

I cough, I shuffle, look left, then right,
As if the door holds my heart in fright.
With every word that chokes my throat,
I just pretend I can't seem to float.

The chair stays warm where stories spun,
While laughter echoes, oh, what fun.
Yet here I stand, my heart on the line,
Hoping goodbyes come with a punchline.

So I'll make my exit, with flair and a grin,
And promise you'll see me—you all know when.
For unsaid farewells come wrapped in love,
With winks and chuckles from up above.

Moments Enshrined in Dust

In corners lie the relics of time,
Each dust mote dances, a playful rhyme.
A teddy bear with a chipped-out grin,
Who's heard all my secrets since I was thin.

The old lamp flickers, like it has jokes,
With shadows that crackle and beckon folks.
It whispers warmth, a soft golden hue,
While I find laughter in things I knew.

Old magazines, with colors so bright,
Shelf life expired, but what a delight!
They tell of fashions and old fads once hot,
Now chuckled at in a living room spot.

So let the dust settle, it's here that we find,
Moments of laughter, so sweetly entwined.
Embrace the past, as we gather and share,
In this cozy nook, love fills the air.

Lullabies of the Familiar

Soft whispers from the couch,
Tickling toes as they slouch.
The cat's snore is a lullaby,
While we laugh and wonder why.

Pizza boxes dance with glee,
Old sitcoms on TV spree.
Remotes lost, treasures beneath,
In this mess, we find our wreath.

Parental tales spill on the floor,
Like old toys we can't ignore.
"Remember this?" we guffaw loud,
In silliness we feel so proud.

Socks mixed with the dance of fate,
Buried treasures under the weight.
Here's the humor in yearning days,
Where love is wrapped in playful ways.

Footfalls of Yesterday

Footsteps sneaking by the hall,
Mysteries on the wall.
"Is that you, or the old floor?"
The ghost of snacks we can't ignore.

The fridge hums a cozy tune,
With leftovers much too June.
Laugh lines gather by the bites,
Sharing joy on forgotten nights.

Bouncing chairs make a scene,
Hiding secrets, lost and keen.
Old records skip in distant glee,
As we sway, so wild and free.

Hats and shoes in random pairs,
Stories woven through our hairs.
With every trip and silly sway,
We dance the past into today.

Light Through the Window

Sunbeams playing tag with dust,
In this room, we laugh and trust.
Curtains dance to a gentle breeze,
With every whisper, memories tease.

Coffee cups like old friends,
As the morning softens bends.
"What did you say?" a barked reply,
With giggles stuck in the butterfly.

The cat leaps, dramatic flair,
Chasing shadows without a care.
The clock ticks with a silly grin,
Time warps when love rushes in.

As evening falls, we close the light,
Tales of laughter paint the night.
Under stars, the old songs bloom,
In our hearts, there's always room.

Kindred Spirits Awakened

Voices echo through the night,
As moonlight shines, we take flight.
Pajama parties in the den,
With snacks galore, let's do it again.

Candles flicker with a wink,
Sharing dreams as we clink.
Jokes tumble like popcorn kernels,
In this space, love eternally swirls.

Old board games recall the past,
Laughter echoes, nothing's cast.
"Your turn!" a playful dare,
In this chaos, hearts laid bare.

As pillows find their rightful place,
In this living room, we embrace.
With giggles sweet and spirits bright,
Every moment feels just right.

Unfolding Narratives

In the corner, dust bunnies dance,
Sprinkling laughter in their prance.
A cat on the couch, a king in his throne,
Chasing shadows, never alone.

Old chairs creak like a joke,
As Grandpa share tales of smoke.
Knitting stories with every stitch,
Life's a sitcom, or maybe a glitch.

Cushions dive, a pillow fight,
Mixed-up stories in the fading light.
The fridge hums a comedic tune,
As we plot escapes to the moon.

With spilled tea and playful sighs,
We craft memories, no hard goodbyes.
This room's a stage, we play our part,
Unfolding narratives from the heart.

Reflections in the Glass

The mirror grins with mischief bright,
Reflecting antics late at night.
Socks mispaired, a fashionable rise,
In this gallery of our silly ties.

Coffee spills like a watercolor dream,
Mom's secret recipe—chaos supreme.
Reflections laugh at our crazy quest,
Sorting through laughter, we're truly blessed.

Windows wide with a view of cheer,
As nieces and nephews draw near.
Their giggles bounce, in playful flight,
A symphony of joy, oh what a sight!

With every frame, a snapshot's caught,
In the chaos of love, we find what we sought.
Each glass reveals a joyful dance,
In this living space, we take our chance.

Conversations of Heart and Home

Pillow talk with sprightly flair,
Whiskers peek from the fire's glare.
Words tumble like kittens at play,
In the den where we spend our day.

Laughter crackles like electric air,
Trading secrets, we banish despair.
The couch giggles under our weight,
In this room, we wholeheartedly create.

Board games sprawled, a battlefield in sight,
Who's winning? It's all in good light.
Cheeky banter, mismatched socks roam,
Conversations spark, we've found our home.

As dusk falls, the stories ignite,
Heartfelt musings bathe in twilight.
In every word, and every jest,
These moments of laughter, we're truly blessed.

Paths Crossed Again

Footprints shuffle on the worn-out rug,
Spilling popcorn, a playful hug.
Time bends as we gather round,
In this maze of laughter, friends are found.

The old clock ticks with a knowing grin,
Tales of mischief starting to spin.
Chasing our shadows on the wall,
Paths crossed again, we answer the call.

An old guitar strums a nostalgic tune,
Dance like nobody's watching, not even the moon.
Outrageous stories ignite our night,
And with each laugh, we take flight.

As chairs squeak, and walls lean in,
We celebrate where we've all been.
In this gathering, love brightly beams,
Paths crossed again, we weave our dreams.

Conversations with Yesterday

A chair creaks under my weight,
Old ghosts in the cushions wait.
They chuckle at my clumsy stance,
Reminding me of that silly dance.

The clock ticks with a cheeky grin,
As I recall the mess I've been.
My socks are mismatched, what a sight,
Was I in a hurry or just too bright?

Laughter bubbles up from the fridge,
Leftovers whisper, 'Come take a bridge.'
I peek inside, an old stew stares back,
A culinary mishap, a flavor hack.

In this room, the past takes flight,
In pots and pans and morning light.
Every corner holds a delight,
Where yesterday teases with sheer insight.

Tones of the Everyday

The broom dances on its own today,
Whilst dust bunnies roll out to play.
Do they know they're quite a sight?
A furry party in morning light!

The coffee pot hums a jazzy tune,
While mugs hold secrets, like a boon.
A spoon clinks softly, quite the star,
Stirring up laughter from near and far.

The curtains sway to a silent song,
Where socks travel as if they belong.
I find a pair, mismatched and bold,
A fashion trend lost in a tale of old.

A cat meows tunes of ancient lore,
As he expertly claims the floor.
His head's held high, a regal show,
In the symphony of our household flow.

When the Fire Flickers

The flames are chatterboxes, flickering bright,
They share tales of the wood's last fight.
Smoke curls up with a wink and a laugh,
As memories dance in the fireplace's path.

The marshmallows giggle, wait for their turn,
While forks jostle in a game of burn.
A s'more here, a cocoa flow,
Taste buds play tag, go with the flow.

Ghost stories tumble from the shelf,
Each creature is a memory of a former self.
Walls lean in to hear the delight,
As shadows perform in the soft golden light.

Beneath the hearth, secrets lie deep,
In every crack, in every leap.
When the fire flickers and the laughter rolls,
The room fills up with our shared souls.

Faint Voices in the Quiet

The fridge hums softly, a lullaby sweet,
Whispers of snacks, a tasty retreat.
I'm convinced it knows when I'm near,
Its voice calls, 'Hey, come grab a beer!'

Dust motes dance in the afternoon sun,
Playing hide-and-seek, oh what fun!
They giggle as I wave my hand,
Agreeing to a game so unplanned.

The couch sighs with stories untold,
Where laughter rings out, fierce and bold.
Each cushion holds a plan, a dream,
In the chorus of our living room theme.

As silence settles, the clock strikes three,
Its tick-tock pulse flows endlessly.
Yet faint voices in the quiet plead,
'Come join our fun, fulfill the need!'

Dreamscapes of Autumn Evenings

Socks mismatched, but who will care?
Pies cooling, spices fill the air.
Under the table, the cat snores loud,
While we share dreams of being unbowed.

Ghosts of laughter dance by the fire,
Mismatched chairs, our strange empire.
The heater sputters, a comedic tune,
As we plot our escape to the moon.

Leaves outside are doing the jig,
Conversations twirling, getting big.
Cupcakes fly, oh what a mess!
Whipped cream battles? We must confess!

Timid ghosts might want to join,
But our antics have them all disown.
So we sip cider, winks abound,
In this haven, joy is found.

A Canvas of Silent Moments

A canvas draped in colors bright,
Hidden treasures in morning light.
The couch a ship in laughter's tide,
We sail on jokes that we can't hide.

Pillows fluffed, a fortress built,
As we wage war with our silly guilt.
Snack attacks are on the way,
While shadows recoil, we laugh and play.

The clock strikes twelve, what a delight!
Still we linger, sugar-fueled flight.
Justice served in tickling rounds,
Sparks of joy in rib-tickling sounds.

Whispers bounce with giggles' charm,
In our bubble, the world feels warm.
We sketch out tales both bold and bright,
In this realm, everything feels right.

Tapestries of Memory Lining the Walls

We hang our quirks like art on walls,
With every laugh, a new thread calls.
Photos frame us in wild poses,
Caught mid-laughter, God only knows.

Tea spills over, a comedy show,
As the dog jumps up, stealing the flow.
A tumble here, a laugh escapes,
We weave our fate in silly shapes.

Mismatched socks and stories told,
With each sip, our antics unfold.
The grace of moments we can't afford,
In this dance, the chaos roared.

With every knick-knack, a tale we share,
Crafted laughter hangs in the air.
Our humble home, a place to roam,
Where joy is the only true tome.

The Heartbeat of a Forgotten Space

In a corner chair, a sock puppet sighs,
Feigning wisdom, with crooked eyes.
Dust bunnies swirl in solo dance,
While we plot pranks, fueled by chance.

The fridge hums an old, familiar tune,
As we debate the best movie cartoon.
A misplaced spoon, an ice cream quest,
Takes us to heights we know the best.

Laughter bubbles in the air like tea,
Flying stories as wild as can be.
Old board games spread like a map,
In this haven, there's barely a gap.

The sun sets low, a golden fade,
Our silliness is never delayed.
With secrets kept and smiles exchanged,
In this forgotten space, all is rearranged.

Distant Sirens of Comfort

In the corner, a chair that creaks,
Muffled laughter from the fridge that leaks.
The cat looks at me like I'm the fool,
Shenanigans unfold, breaking every rule.

The clock ticks loud, each second a jest,
Time for snacks, let's put it to the test.
Remote in hand, I'm the couch potato,
Reality show? Just my old potato.

The pizza box waves, a crunchy delight,
Glimpses of joy in the late-night light.
Neighbors' parties blare like a siren's song,
But here on the sofa, I feel I belong.

And when the doorbell rings late after ten,
It's just my imagination, starting again.
With each little noise, my giggles expand,
In this zany realm, I'm the ruler unplanned.

Dappled Light and Shadows

Sunbeams dance over the cluttered floor,
While shadows chase dust bunnies to the door.
A sock on the mantle, where's the other pair?
Life's little chaos, a treasure most rare.

The dog's on the couch, watching TV with glee,
Barking at heroes, oh, how can this be?
A sippy cup gathered dust on the side,
A relic from parties with laughter and pride.

The plants seem to whisper secrets untold,
Recounting adventures of nights brave and bold.
With the flick of a switch, lights dimmed down low,
Even the cushions have stories to show.

And I sit with my book, a sip of sour tea,
Half-amused at the world, so odd yet carefree.
The living room buzzes with energy bright,
In this tangled joy, everything feels right.

Tidal Waves of Memories

In every corner, tales wash ashore,
Of moments forgotten—like socks, ten more!
The TV flickers with a gleaming glow,
While laughter rises like tides, ebb and flow.

Old photos hang, the smiles frozen in time,
Silly grins captured, a visual rhyme.
The ice cream stains on the couches remind,
Of parties where fun never fell far behind.

Beneath all the clutter, a treasure chest lies,
Of board games and crayons, all for surprise.
Prized trophies from battles in pixelated lands,
And cookie crumbs scattered like forgotten bands.

A tapestry woven of giggles and woes,
The magic of youth in each wrinkle that grows.
Tidal waves crash as I sink in my chair,
In this living room treasure, I find my flair.

The Soft Brush of Time

Tick-tock and twist, the clock has a laugh,
Mismatched timers for a hilarious path.
Cushions rearrange in their comfy old way,
Like a family reunion that drags out the day.

Laughter spills over like coffee too hot,
Mom's secret recipe ends up in a pot.
The smell wafts through, it's a culinary thrill,
Even the fridge whispers, "Good luck, choke down that swill!"

The cable's gone wild, always searching for gold,
Dramas unfolding, so tragically bold.
Remote in a battle, the dog's won the steal,
But I cuddle the cat, sharing secrets surreal.

With a glance at the door, the dog leaps with cheer,
While the world outside fades, it's clear, oh so clear.
In this soft brush of time, absurdity reigns,
Inside our warm bubble, where laughter remains.

Unheard Notes of Togetherness

In the corner lies a chair,
A relic from times we did share.
Socks and cushions in a pile,
Whispers of laughter, quite a while.

A remote stuck under the couch,
We find it, but still, we slouch.
Popcorn flies with every film,
Faces bright, the joy we brim.

Cats plotting on the window sill,
While we argue - who gets the grill?
Forgotten snacks beneath the dust,
In this chaos, we place our trust.

So much noise, yet silence too,
Grumpy boots and jolly crew.
Together here, it's all so bright,
Our living room is pure delight!

Melancholy in the Milieu

The plants are thriving, well, somewhat,
But that TV? It's really shot!
In the midst of tangled wires,
Memory foam and curious fires.

Chairs that squeak like old-time tales,
While snacks are dropped in hushed fails.
Dust bunnies dance on wooden floors,
Chasing each other through open doors.

Odd socks peeking from the void,
Did you lose it? Oh, how we're annoyed!
Yet laughter pricks that silent space,
We carry this charm, this funny race.

Cushions staged like night-time dreams,
Flexibility's torn at the seams.
In this chaos, we find our peace,
And what's a mess, but fun's increase!

Resounding Memories

The clock ticks loud, beats like a drum,
Sipping tea while we chew some gum.
Sticky fingers on the couch,
Jokes fly fast and laughter crouch.

Cards scattered around like fallen leaves,
Somehow our skill is what it deceives.
Games that end in a childish fight,
Yet we'll hug it out, make it right.

Old albums stacked in disarray,
Faded memories wrap us in play.
We click the camera, a silly pose,
Our quirks, our quirks, everyone knows!

In this room, our hearts do roar,
Who knew chaos could be such a score?
Here's to the space that holds our cheer,
In every corner, love's frontier!

Vibrations of the Mundane

Feet up on the table, a slouchy scene,
Every snack odd, and the drinks obscene.
Flats on display, a circus in sight,
We trip on shoes, and that's our plight.

Chasing echoes of voices sweet,
While doing battle with defeat.
The comic books piled high, in a tower,
As we laugh softly, in this timeless hour.

Argument over whose turn to choose,
In this room, we always lose.
Snore from the dog, a soft lullaby,
While the world outside zips by.

Memory quilts stitched with grace,
We embrace the rhythm of our space.
Every moment, both weird and grand,
In the backdrop of life, we stand!

The Old Record Player Speaks

Round and round, it spins with sass,
Dusty tunes from a vintage past.
Grooves like grandma's dance moves,
Chasing cat with rhythm fast.

Whispers of time, it clicks and pops,
As I search for memories, it never stops.
A little scratch, a little hiss,
A symphony of songs I thought I'd miss.

With every crackle, laughter unfolds,
Tales of trips to places bold.
Spinning stories of my old pet,
In a melody I won't forget.

A rabbit hole of beats and cheer,
As I twirl to tunes from yesteryear.
It's a concert of chaos, a lively scene,
The old record player, my time machine.

Nostalgia's Gentle Caress

Cushions fluffed, and worn-out seats,
Where stories dance in hushed retreats.
The sun pours in, like a golden brew,
As I reminisce, the laughter grew.

Old photos smile with a cheeky grin,
Reminding me of where I've been.
Mismatched socks like quirky art,
A mismatched life that stole my heart.

Whispers linger like the scent of pie,
Crumbly crusts that almost fly.
Every corner holds a joke untold,
In the living room, memories unfold.

Tickles and giggles in the corners stay,
As nostalgia beckons and leads the way.
With every glance, a tale will sprout,
In this lively room, there's no doubt.

The Melodies of Muffled Silence

A hush that tells a lively tale,
Of Netflix fests and snacks on sale.
The couch squeaks like a laugh at night,
As secrets hide, then take to flight.

In every corner, mischief lies,
Underneath the watchful eyes.
A blanket fort of dreams and schemes,
Where giggles break and courage beams.

Leftover pizza, a silent feast,
With crusty humor that won't cease.
When silence speaks, the jokes abound,
In every heartbeat, laughter's found.

The remote's lost, again it seems,
A mystery that haunts my dreams.
Yet in this room, it's crystal clear,
Muffled silence still brings cheer.

Heartbeats Beneath the Surface

Under layers of laughter lies,
Tickling hearts, oh how time flies!
A coffee cup, with a witty grin,
Echoing thoughts tucked deep within.

A cat that naps in vibrant light,
Dreams of mice and a daring flight.
As I shuffle through my cozy pile,
Every heartbeat brings a smile.

Poking fun at all my woes,
With every joke, a friendship grows.
Vaudeville beats in this cozy space,
Where silliness wears a friendly face.

Beneath the surface, giggles thrive,
In the mess of life, we feel alive.
With every beat of joy that's shared,
In this lively room, we are unpaired.

Whispers of Forgotten Memories

In the corner, a cat naps soundly,
While crumbs dance like ghosts around me.
A chair creaks with secrets kept,
And I wonder what stories it has wept.

Old photos grin from the wall above,
The smiles frozen, a memory glove.
Laughter spills from a distant place,
As I step over dust that holds a trace.

A plant droops, its leaves in despair,
Reminds me of my last poor care.
Socks are mismatched, a comical sight,
Who knew laundry could spark a fight?

Yet here I sit with a grin that's wide,
These whispers of joy I can't abide.
In this cozy nook, I find delight,
With memories dancing in the soft twilight.

Shadows of Unspoken Words

The toaster pops, a breakfast cheer,
While shadows flicker, drawing near.
A sock puppet speaks in a jumbled tongue,
As I ponder where my keys have hung.

Coffee stains map a wild route,
To a treasure where lost thoughts pursue.
A vacuum glares like a jealous foe,
Why can't it just let the old crumbs go?

Balloons from last year's party spree,
Float low and whisper secrets to me.
The fridge hums a lazy tune,
In this lively mess, I can't help but swoon.

With laughter lurking in every nook,
I chase the echoes like a silly crook.
In this space filled with jest so absurd,
Life's candid moments are shared with a word.

Reflections in the Faded Light

A lamp flickers, casting strange forms,
As dust bunnies dance in subtle swarms.
The couch sighs, accommodating my weight,
While snacks vanish, as if on a fate.

Frames askew tell tales long gone,
Of neighbors' chickens and lawn ornaments drawn.
A bowl of forgotten fruit sits shy,
How did that apple learn to fly?

The dog snores loudly, a rhythm beats,
A perfect soundtrack as laughter repeats.
I trip on the rug, it's a hazardous bait,
Yet this living room feels just first-rate.

With every glance, a new story ignites,
The faded light contains funny sights.
In this patchwork haven, both cozy and bright,
I cherish the quirks that drift into night.

Voices Beneath the Ceiling

Upstairs, there's thumping, a curious sound,
Is it a dance or just kids fooling around?
The clock ticks loudly, marking the time,
While I ponder if life's a big rhyme.

Cushing plops and flops down on the floor,
As I mutter about chaos and chores galore.
What was once neat is a playful mess,
Cushions with crumbs, it's anyone's guess.

A spider spins tales in delicate threads,
Whispering secrets while I dodge my bed.
The remote's gone missing, the dog winks sly,
Oh, the mischief that happens when I go awry!

Yet amidst the ruckus, I can't complain,
For every mishap brings joy just the same.
With laughter booming from above my bones,
This madcap living room feels like home.

Unraveled Threads of Togetherness

In a room full of laughter, we read the same book,
But somehow, you skipped to the last page, it took!
Spoilers unwrapped, like gifts from old years,
The punchlines land softly, through giggles and cheers.

Cousins play charades, dramatic and bold,
But Uncle throws a fit, 'That's not what I told!'
The cat looks bewildered, as if to convey,
That family antics are quite a buffet.

A game of old stories, the blunders retold,
Each tale getting taller, a sight to behold.
With each little mishap, we roll in the floor,
And promise next week, we just won't bring more!

Yet here we are gathered, with snacks in our hands,
Replaying the moments that life never planned.
In this cozy chaos, so much love we find,
In threads of our stories, all tangled but kind.

The Breath of Familiar Faces

When the door swings open, and faces appear,
We wave and we grin, with laughter sincere.
Grandma's got cookies, but also some jokes,
Her punchlines, more crumby than all of her folks.

Aunt Sally's new dance, it's something to see,
She twirls and she spins, oh dear, let it be!
With every mishap, a snort here and there,
Keeps our spirits soaring, a joy we all share.

Dad's trying to cook, but the smoke's rising high,
"Is it a roast or a fire?" we all wink and sigh.
Yet amidst all the chaos, the warmth takes its place,
In the quirky expanse of each familiar face.

With games and old photos, we fill up the night,
Stories of yesterdays, from left-handed bites.
Through laughter and gaffes, our hearts intertwine,
In this merry madness, everything feels fine.

Beneath the Surface

We gather like fish in a splendid fishbowl,
Beneath surface laughter, our quirks take a stroll.
With winks and with nudges, we swap silly tales,
Confessions come easy, our humor never fails.

There's Aunt Claire's old recipe that missed the mark,
It's sweet, it's sour, and oh, what a lark!
She stirs up the chaos with flair and with zest,
"Next time," she chuckles, "I'll just order the rest!"

The family debates if it's pizza or pies,
We argue in jest 'neath the faraway skies.
Every comment brings wiggles, a chorus of glee,
Who knew all it took was a dip in the sea?

And beneath all the banter, a truth shines so bright,
That love is the laughter, the heart of the night.
With each silly moment, we deepen our ties,
In the whirlpool of joy, we're all deep in spies.

Time Lingers

Time lingers the way that old cheese does smell,
In a room filled with stories we know all too well.
Each second a snapshot, of fun and of cheer,
As we plot our next mishap, the next grand idea.

With a laugh and a wink, we reroute the game,
There's always a wild card in family's name.
Silly hats and props, oh, the chaos we sow,
Time's but a backdrop to the fun that we grow.

The clock keeps on ticking, but we hardly care,
With hearts on our sleeves, and crumbs everywhere.
We dance through the chaos like children at play,
Making memories that will never decay.

Though the minutes may scatter and fade into night,
In this world of our making, we've set all things right.
Forever and always, these moments we keep,
In the laughter of family, our hearts take a leap.

Windows to Our Yesterdays

In every cracked window, a scene comes alive,
Of birthdays and picnics where laughter would thrive.
We're actors in stories, each role plays a part,
From the mischief of youth to wise tales at heart.

The couch isn't just furniture; it's where we reside,
Revisiting moments we just cannot hide.
Quips fly like paper planes, one after another,
As we reminisce on our dear crazy mother.

Those photos on the wall, with faces aglow,
They witness our laughter, the highs and the low.
With squints and with grins, we recount all the fun,
Through the windows of time, our memories run.

So we toast with our mugs, to the years that have flown,
In the living room chaos, we've truly grown.
Each story a treasure, each laugh like a song,
In the windows of yesterday, we find where we belong.

The Rapture of Recollection

In the corner, dust bunnies dance,
Gathering whispers of a long-lost chance.
The sock that vanished, a silent scream,
Underneath the couch, it plots and schemes.

Old sitcoms flicker, laughter on repeat,
Where the punchlines linger, bittersweet.
A remote control lies like a sleeping beast,
Harnessing chaos, it feeds the feast.

Sticky notes cling with messages of glee,
'Wash the dishes' and 'Don't forget me!'
Banana peels slip through the afternoon haze,
As time takes a bow in its silly, silly ways.

So we chuckle at shadows, twist on a chair,
Finding joy in the mess, without a care.
The rapture of memory floats on the breeze,
In our troupe of oddities, we find our ease.

Glimmers of the Unseen

A light switch hangs with a cheeky grin,
Flipping between brightness and shadows, a spin.
The cat plays confetti with bits of old string,
While I ponder the virtues of not being king.

A creaky chair sings a familiar tune,
Like an old friend who just missed the moon.
I swear the lamp winked, it's just my mind,
Or perhaps it's the wine? Never quite blind.

Reflections of chaos spark up on screens,
As the popcorn pops with its glorious scenes.
The walls lean in close, secrets to share,
And I swear the curtains just lifted a hair.

The sunbeams giggle, tickling the floor,
As the dust motes dance in a wild encore.
Together, we revel, the unseen brigade,
In ribbons of laughter, our worries cascade.

Imprints of Love and Loss

On the table, crumbs of yesterday's feast,
A battle of forks, oh such a wild beast!
The chair's got a squeak that's almost a tune,
Reminding me sweetly of lavender June.

Old love letters curl in forgotten drawers,
As I sip my tea, daydream through the walls.
The clock ticks a rhythm, both slow and so fast,
Chronicles of laughter, shadows that last.

A mismatched set of mugs, sipping despair,
One reads 'Dream Big,' while the other just stares.
Memories are painted in colors so bright,
Yet slip through the fingers like twilight's light.

So let's toast to the laughter, the silly parade,
To whimsical losses that never quite fade.
In the gallery of time, we hang our delight,
Charmed by the echoes that dance through the night.

Interludes of the Mundane

Dust swirls like ballet dancers on pause,
While I fumble for keys with theatrical flaws.
The fridge hums a song, perhaps it's a joke,
As the leftovers plot, I'll never revoke.

Mugs stacked like towers on the kitchen sink,
A fortress of chaos, my time to rethink.
Laundry baskets overflow with a cheerful grin,
Each sock a witness, oh where have you been?

Vacuum cleaner roars like a dragon on fight,
While crumbs play hide-and-seek, out of sight.
The calendar chuckles, days bouncing along,
As ordinary moments create a new song.

In this circus of daily, we twirl and we sway,
Finding joy in the mess, at the end of the day.
Life's interludes wonder, a comedic spin,
Savoring each chaos, where laughter begins.

The Chorus of Whispers in the Corner

In the corner, secrets hold,
With laughter spun from tales retold.
A sock puppet dons a funny hat,
While the cat, a judge, sits there, so fat.

Grandma's stories bring giggles in waves,
Of her lost shoe and how she misbehaves.
The lamp nods along to the tales that float,
And the cushions chuckle, now taking note.

A sneeze erupts, and the room erupts,
As the dog plots how to sneak and disrupt.
"Please don't eat the couch!" we all squeal,
While fish in the bowl share their own appeal.

All the echoes dance in the light,
Making shadows spin with newfound delight.
For in this room, laughter rings clear,
Where silliness thrives, it's our favorite cheer.

Yesterday's Embrace Still Warming the Air.

Last night's pizza crumbs still remain,
As we recall the movie's insane.
My friend fell asleep, with popcorn on face,
A pillow fort built in our favorite place.

The blanket fort's still a place of dreams,
Where giggles burst like vibrant streams.
We toyed with the idea of flying away,
Yet here we stay, where joy finds a way.

A flying potato was the real star,
As it zoomed within a snickering bazaar.
In this cozy nook, time seems to freeze,
With whispers and laughter carried by breeze.

The warmth lingers on, a hug in the air,
Our stories remain, with splashes of flair.
Here's to the silliness of yesteryear,
Where memories stick and hearts hold dear.

Whispers of the Hearth

By the fire, secrets glean,
With marshmallows singing, oh so serene.
The chair rocks back with a creaky sigh,
While the clock ticks on with a winking eye.

Chips dance on the table with glee,
As the dog thinks he's part of the spree.
We laugh about that time we were brave,
Dared to swim in the neighbor's wave.

Stories of ghosts who eat toast at night,
And the strange sock that took a flight.
In this cozy nook, humor ignites,
While shadows play silly tricks in the lights.

The night winds down, but giggles will stay,
In the warmth of our hearts, they'll never stray.
Farewell for now to this riotous mirth,
Till we gather again by the fire's hearth.

Shadows on Soft Upholstery

On plush couches, shadows waltz,
With mischief lurking, never a fault.
A bowl of snacks, a curious cat,
And giggles spread where the soft beams sat.

A twist of fate with a jump and a leap,
Where friends collide in a heap of sheep.
We play charades, though no one can tell,
If our moves are grace or a joyful farewell.

The funky rug holds mischievous dreams,
With squishy finales and silly themes.
We chase the giggles that frolic around,
While mismatched cushions bounce to the sound.

In every crack and crevice, joy nestles tight,
With echoes of laughter that feel just right.
So here's to the moments, absurd in their glee,
Where shadows dance wildly, forever carefree.

The Aura of the Abiding

In the corner, a sock does hide,
An old book then comes to bide.
Couch cushions bestow their grace,
While a cat claims her resting place.

Laughter rings from jars of jam,
As a playful dog greets the fam.
Spilled snacks and crumbs align,
Who knew chaos could be so divine?

The clock ticks, a rhythm so bold,
Whispers of stories yet untold.
A game of charades begins anew,
With a flourish and a ridiculous cue!

And then the prankster starts to scheme,
Filling the room with giggles and dream.
Comical chaos, a joyful spree,
This is how life's meant to be!

Light Through the Doorway

Sunbeams dance with playful light,
Chasing shadows, oh what a sight.
A tumbleweed rolls across the floor,
And the laughter spills out the door.

A chair squeaks, it creaks and groans,
A cat yawns, it stretches and moans.
Brightened by sunlight in a gleam,
Caught in whimsical, daydream schemes.

The kettle whistles, a comical tune,
While spoons do the tango in the noon.
Sips of tea that welcome a chuckle,
Life here feels like one big huddle.

Light beams twist in the playful air,
Turning moments into delightful flair.
Every corner hums a refrain,
Echoing joy, like a sweet champagne!

Unexpected Visits of Thought

Silly musings swirl around,
A sock thinks it's lost and found.
Dancing thoughts in twilight's glow,
Like confetti, off they go!

A microwave hums a secret tune,
While dust bunnies to the beat attune.
Potato chips crunch like laughter's call,
Crackers crumble, and they fall.

The mailman drops a funny note,
Saying he's seen a singing goat.
Imagining a world so bizarre,
Where pizzas fly and cows are stars!

With each whimsy, giggles grow,
Painting bright smiles on the flow.
In this realm of silly thoughts,
Life serves up whatever it's got!

Shadows Dancing in the Twilight

In the evening, shadows grow bold,
Twisting and turning with tales of old.
A broomstick hosts the comical crew,
As they glide like they've nothing to do.

The sofa giggles with muffled cheer,
As old cartoons draw us near.
Chasing shadows in the fading light,
With the laughter that feels just right.

A dance party breaks in the gloom,
As the lamp vaudevilles, lighting the room.
Cups and plates sing the waltz of fun,
While twinkling stars join, everyone!

So here we are, in twilight's embrace,
Where shadows laugh and time finds its pace.
In this living room, mischief reigns,
As joy springs forth in playful chains!

www.ingramcontent.com/pod-product-compliance
Lightning Source LLC
Chambersburg PA
CBHW062112280426
43661CB00086B/521